Rūḥ

Zummar F. Ansari

Illustrated by Zaynab Waqas

Cover by Ibad Nasir

authorHOUSE®

AuthorHouse™ UK
1663 Liberty Drive
Bloomington, IN 47403 USA
www.authorhouse.co.uk
Phone: 0800.197.4150

Published by AuthorHouse   12/13/2017

ISBN: 978-1-5462-8030-9 (sc)
ISBN: 978-1-5462-8029-3 (e)

Library of Congress Control Number: 2017915479

Contents

Orphic

Wishful 1

Polaroid 3

Insaan 5

Look Back 7

Always 12

Lover, Be Careful 15

Unpleasant Pleasantries 17

Fallacy 19

Tzu 21

No One Is Truly Lost in the Presence of Art 23

Name of the Game 28

Tilikum 30

Phobia 32

Warm Heart 34

Youthful 36

Unfathomed 38

Loyalty to the Motherland 40

Cynical 42

Nothing Above You 44

The Unsaid 46

Wings 48

Afterthoughts 50

Shams 52

Joseph 54

The Principal Paradox 56

Letters from Konya 58

Winehouse 60

Oracle 62

An Antipode Epiphany 64

Validity 66

Intimidatory 68

Thank You 70

Slavery 72

Figment 74

Embryo 76

Letting Go 78

Fulfilments 80

Everything and Nothing 82

Molten Marble 84

Expiry 86

Confines 88

Why 90

Provenience 92

Kalopsia

Caves 96

The Last Hour 98

Elementary 103

Delinquent 105

My Demise 107

Black Eden 111

Intellectual Conversations with a Whimsical Biologist 115

Stars in Every Darkness Save Our Own 117

Element 119

Cloudless 121

Tetrodotoxin 123

Itch 125

Frame of Reference 127
Syria.. 129
For Maggie Steber..................................... 131
To My First and Last King................................. 133
The Audacity of Beauty II 135
Indoctrination.. 137
For Hyb 139
Tomorrow We Fight Again 142
Explication... 145
Breaking 149
Decorum...151
Rubies 153
Endurance... 157
Idle... 159
Expressing the Inexpressible.............................. 161
You Cannot Give What You Do Not Have.......... 163
Letters from Johannesburg................................. 165
Echo... 167
Realism 169
Precedence 171
Underestimated... 173
Verdict 175
Solace... 177
Selfish 179
The Self.. 183
"And Never Is Your Lord Forgetful" [19:64] 185
Dimension 4 187
Cages on the Trees of Heaven 189
Native 191
Limits 193

Glorious

The Loudest Most Peaceful Silence I Know 197
Inborn.. 199

Flurry...201

Abstract 203

Fingerprints 205

Unadulterated 207

For Letting Us In...209

Purpose...211

I Won't Tell a Soul 213

Little Mighty 215

Origins..218

Damaged Goods..220

Ruins 222

Genuine..224

War of Words...226

Polar..228

Painful Loyalty 232

Test..234

The Cosmos in Me..238

Intrepid...241

Conflict...243

Hijab..245

A Tragedy 247

Powerless...249

Ringleader...251

Metaphorical..253

Pandemonium..257

More 259

Like a Clay Pigeon 261

J. 263

Letters from Mexico..265

Letters from a Durrani......................................269

Glad You Left 271

Letters from Constantinople 273

Letters from Balochistan 275

Gravitation...277

What Have We Done..279

Just Don't Forget Your Roots 282

Forgiveness..284

Not All the Broken Need Saving...........................288

Slates...294

Scarcity 298

Blue Sky...300

Ultimate Consumer 303

Totka 305

Prowess 309

Allegiance 311

Across the River 316

Trust Not the Words of Poets 318

Predators...322

Floodgates...324

Miranda...326

Flounders...328

The June Riots 330

Brown Lake 332

The Promise 336

Logastellus 338

Knitting..342

Afterword 346

For the love of God

Know that
victory comes
with patience,
relief with affliction,
and ease with
hardship

–Muhammad

To my readers,

In times of great confusion and unrest, I have found that peace lies in the words both of scripture and of mortal origins. I have so much respect and admiration for those artists and poets who have shared their work with the world so that we may be reminded that we are not alone on this path.

As human beings, we often fail to identify complex emotions or even know that they exist within us. And that is where the art comes in. Whether in paint or ink or voice, art expresses the inexpressible. It identifies what is present in us and what is absent and, most significantly, what needs healing.

To those artists and to those poets, thank you for teaching me that pain does not have to be in vain, that pain can be used not to build walls but to build bridges.

And so forth, I have compiled my own words into this book so that they may resonate in the hearts of people I have never even met – an opportunity and honour that I cannot begin to express my gratitude for. I hope my words consume your voids and make you feel a little less fragmentary, as they have done for me.

If my words become a source of inspiration for you, dear reader, please do not hesitate to take your own complexities and make a declaration of their presence.

I say this so that our art may reach the most desolate corners of Earth and teach lost souls of the freedom that comes with expression.

With the utmost love,

Zummar F. Ansari

Orphic

Wishful

In the midst of this
hate and blood,

it gives me so much
peace (and far more
hope) in knowing that
the bad sometimes
resent their evil and

wish to change.

Polaroid

maybe we love the old
and the forgotten
because, deep down,
we know all too well
that just like them we
will expire too.

Insaan

All you needed was a
little reminder that being
the abuser is not the only
way not to be abused.

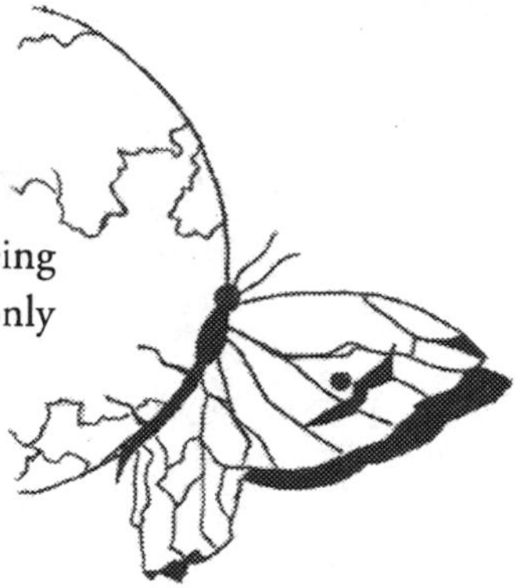

Look Back

When we reminisce about our childhoods,
we don't remember sequences or stories –
we remember feelings;
we remember glimpses;
we remember sounds
of fragmented memories.

Reminisce.

The things that stuck around were the ones
that left a mark, affected you one way (or the other).

•

I remember my father.

When we crossed the road, he always
walked on the side of the oncoming traffic
so that his bones would break first if any were to.

It was one gesture. Now I see it in every choice I make.

If you feel a little lost (or completely),
if you feel like a stranger in your own skin,

look back.

(The things that stayed will speak to you;
they'll let you in on the secrets of your identity.)

If you remember darkness,
rise from the ashes – tall and strong.

If you remember standing on top of mountains,
start reaching for the vastness above them.

But, dear reader, please remember:

do not drown in pride;
do not drown in pity.

Caged birds
sing the loudest.

Always

I have always been
The girl with little hands
and little feet.

But then their voices
rose at you.

And suddenly, I was not
small anymore.

There was a fire that
roared in my chest, and
beautiful fury surged
through my blood.

You were silent –
patient and graceful,
as always.

But God didn't give you
Me for my patience or

My graceful silence.

Protect you, I will –
with blood,
with love,

always.

Lover, Be Careful

When you
hold someone
dear and near, you have started playing with fire.

Lover, be careful what you utter,
of what you do,
of what you think.

For ultimately, we find refuge
in places we feel safe –
places where we are accepted.

So be careful. Be the safe havens.
If not, they will slip out of your reach
    like dust through fingers.

You won't see it. You won't know it.

You will feel it.

But only when it's gone.

Lover, be careful.

Unpleasant Pleasantries

"I love you
like the waves
love the moon,
but when the
time comes for
sacrifice,
you will
have to
be the one
to surrender."

But I swear I love you.

Fallacy

Like a distant memory
from an obscure past –
and it was only yesterday.

Tzu

Two people – two realms:

One

saw how the tall grass
bent over backwards as
commanded by the wind
and said, "How oppressive
is the air that takes advantage
of she who cannot move nor run!"

The other

smiled and rejoiced with the tall
grass; she had found love that
was worth bending for.
He breathed in her joy and said,
"You have not moved, nor have you
rummaged the Earth for companionship;
you found yourself, and it found you!"

No One Is Truly Lost in the Presence of Art

If you struggle
to see beneath
skin,
beneath the
façade –
don't look at them,
but look at the things
they attach their
identities to.

Look at the art
they admire, at
the colors, at the
brushstrokes;
read the books
they read,
the poetry,
whether they
find comfort
in the noise
or in the silence,
in the words
or in the music.

These mirrors –
use them to see
yourself, too.

But also remember:
the truth is not for
every heart or eye
or ear,
because what is true
is what is raw.
And what is raw is what
is powerful.

And we are weak.

You knew where to tug,
and you didn't hesitate.

Name of the Game

Every attempt at happiness —

        a poem,
        a celebration,
        a painting,
        a song,
        every breath,
        every affiliation,
        every love —

is to distract us from a reality too abominable.

Despite the vastness of this blue planet,

we are irredeemably

alone.

And the height of good fortune

is finding someone who will

make a little room for our

loneliness in their own.

Tilikum

Culture, traditions, history;

like gentle streams of
knowledge and wisdom
from distant lands,

but also like silent killers,
at times bestowing upon us
entities that are better left
forgotten.

I grew up loving the zoo.
It was magic in all its
exotic glory.

But I have seen, and I have heard.

I now look at children marvelling
at caged cuckoos, wishing I could
tell them:

Little fledglings,

there is no beauty in stolen freedom.

Phobia

Everything is so impermanent:

fleeting in retrospect,

almost illusory.

What if we lower the gates
and show them our weaknesses?

What if we lose ourselves
in their midst?

What if we lose sight of everything
earthly and make them our sun?

Only to wake up one morning
and see that we're gazing into
the eyes of a stranger.

Warm Heart

If you look with your eyes,

        you will see a cold face,

    a cold stride, and a cold gaze –

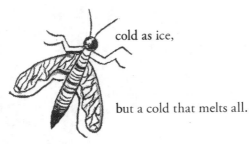

        cold as ice,

        but a cold that melts all.

Youthful

"I am full of life and full of mysteries,"
the ocean cried out. "Yet I have no colour."

The sky heard her melancholy wails below
and offered his own reflection.

Under the sun, she wore his blue and his green
with vast pride.

But under the moon, she succumbed to the night,
reminding herself that without the sky, she was a
mirror that offered no reflections.

Without him, she could not serve her purpose.

Unfathomed

How enigmatic.

When I stood under
the thunder and even
the skies cried with me,
it was then that I felt
the most alone.

Loyalty to the Motherland

Beneath this human hide,
only you see the colors of
the victories of unsung battles.

Let it be your thunder.

Cynical

The air around us is in constant flux.
All the time. I wonder if its mood
changes ours – or is it the contrary?

I wonder if it gets overwhelmed
with all our unsaid (and said) thoughts,
which linger around us, suffocating under the
weight of the seven billion and some.

Or maybe it's not the air that hears.
I'd like to think that some entity knows
us to the core – beneath bone, flesh, and blood.
One that does not get overwhelmed or suffocated
by our endless dire straits.

I'd like to believe there is an entity.
One who remains after the people
turn away or turn to dust.

I would like to believe.

Nothing Above You

How is it that when you
lose someone, instead of
disappearing, they become
a part of everything and
anything?

You catch them lurking in
happy places and sad corners,
in the smiles of others, in
grains of sand,

        in mirrors,

in nothing,   in everything,

nowhere,   everywhere.

Their absence becomes a presence –

vicious as fire to wood,
annihilator of all peace,

        of all quiet,

        of all calm.

The Unsaid

When you're young,
words flow out of
your mouth like rivers,
unquenchable and dauntless.

A little older, you realize that
not everything you utter is
meant for every ear.

A little more, and you realize
you have managed to amass
a collection of words that
carry regret and ache.

The drought takes over.
The river halts.
The unsaid hangs in the air,
desolate and void of hope.

And suddenly, you start to
speak words with caution
for fear of breaking them
and their final destinations.

Wings

It was as **if** you
had given me
wings and made
me a bird;
floods could
drown the earth,
earthquakes
could swallow
it whole, and I,
in the sky, was
safe.

Afterthoughts

My favourite smiles
are those we put on
when we don't think
anyone's looking –

where I catch glimpses
of it etched across your
face, thinking no one
sees,

fleeting yet so fulfilling.

Shams

The sincere are those who
make you realise what you
have been missing all this
time, rather than glorifying
your present existence.

Like mirrors that show you
what is absent rather than
what is present,

they are the forces that move
your stagnant waters towards
the open sea.

Joseph

Your deepest presence
lies in your deepest vulnerabilities.

Let yourself break;
it's the only way light
can flood your insides
through the little cracks
(and the big ones) –

the light that will allow
you to see through the
purples of pain.

Let yourself break
in hopes of a day when
all this carnage will
seem worth it.

The Principal Paradox

The world I live in
stands on pillars
of paradoxes and
metaphors.

The same water
that gives life can
also take it away.

Fire that keeps the
mountain people
warm can also
turn them to
ashes.

Earth from which
we feed –
our gateway to the sun –
can crack open
and swallow us
without warning.

This. This is the artist I want to meet.

Letters from Konya

When I didn't know any better,
I used to rain down on people
with my words.

They sounded so irrefutable in
my mind, and I could not,
for the life of me,
understand how anyone
could see the world through
eyes other than mine.

With wisdom that only
comes with steady aging
and with time,
it became known to me that

the world is changed
by my example,
and not my opinion.

Winehouse

"Listen to your heart," they always throw at us,

ignorant of the fact that most of us choose not
to hear the things we *know* it has to say,

ignorant of the fear of following **what we truly**
love,

for things worth fighting for often **come**
with the possibility of failing to attain them,

and failure of this kind would mean we are
left without purpose.

So sometimes we choose not to listen.

Oracle

Like a blind woman
who sees the sun for
the very first time,
these words had
become light
for me.

So it
was sad when
the deeper I was
falling for them, the
more I realized that they
alone would never fill our voids.

An Antipode Epiphany

A look,
six words,
two morose thoughts,
and a sickening twist of the gut —

seeing through the eyes of a victim,
I had never noticed the oppressor in me,
the part that had always prevailed.

 **Validity**

Don't be sad, don't pretend.

You finally have
something legitimate
to be ungrateful for –

what you always *truly* wanted.

Intimidatory

Funny how they
run even before
we open our mouths
for the second time.

Darling, you haven't
even seen past the
surface.

Thank You

I prayed to God
to show us the
truth,

and He made you
throw us aside
when it was more
convenient than
keeping us.

Slavery

At dusk, as the sky
was ripping apart
to build itself again,
she felt feeling in her legs –

so this is how sovereignty feels?

(Freedom from the confines of minds. Minds.
And hearts. And you. And me.)

Disastrously, my soul knows
it will only take a whiff
of that smell you carry –
on a busy street,
in a corridor,
a shop,
and my legs will
cease to be my own.

I will stand there, aquiver.

Figment

We write poetry when we feel voiceless.
We turn to scripture when we want perspective.
We make art out of ache, we artisans of pain.

But I wonder.

When exactly did we, instead of healing the voids
of our universes, start to accept them and just fill
them with substitutes that will never truly heal us?

When did we stop fighting for ourselves?

Embryo

Take me back to the start –
where stardust and dark matter reigned,
when all what mattered was growth,
and there was no one to stand in our way –

when we were all
born the same.

Letting Go

Give them wings
and let them fly
before your
own creations
start feeding on
she who gave
them life.

Fulfilments

I'll only know I did okay
if I can walk out of this
and be able to say with
all my heart that

there was nothing
more I could've
possibly done.

You ask why
I am always
tired.

This is why.

Everything and Nothing

Actions speak
louder than –

Molten Marble

I had put aside my pride.
I had surrendered to the tide.

I had championed myself

(for you, even when it was
supposed to be for me).

And when I crawled
back to your feet
seeking redemption,

I was no war hero.

I hadn't drowned oceans.

I was still *inadequate*.

You had written me in stone,
and I was never to change.

Expiry

I've been chasing the
past for so long.

Now, I hold it in my
hands, and I know not
what purpose it serves.

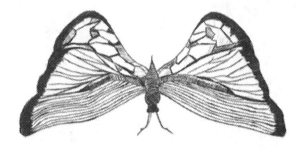

Confines

You built those walls
to keep them out,

but all they ever did
was keep you in.

Why

knowledge, it's a beautiful thing.
Money, power, beauty, people, memories, time –

all fade, betray, disappoint.

The knowledge? It is yours.
Yours to keep. Yours to cherish,
and, most importantly, yours to
give.

The one thing they can not take away.

It is yours. It is yours. It is yours.

Provenience

It's been a long way,
a momentous declaration of
the power of human will,
of human endeavour.

It has not been without strife.
[dark corners]
[dead ends]
[empty promises]
[broken places]
[lies]

But I can finally see the light.
Oh! Darling, it's worth the fight

Here, the wind, he talks of freedom.
I see no birds.
(I think it's because *we* are the birds.)

Regrettably, the map to this haven is not mine to give.

But I can tell you where to start.

Do not give death dominion over life.

You, bearer of the sacred gift, it is the only one you will ever get.

Be kind, be wise.

Kalopsia

Caves

So odd.

When you can see the birds (freedom)
and feel the wind on your face (feeling)
and walk the Earth as you please (wander),

but you've never felt so imprisoned by [_____].

This psychological claustrophobia is your reality,

not the birds,
not the wind,
not the earth –

a prisoner in the midst of such freedom.

The Last Hour

I remember that morning.
It was orange and
yellow in the middle.
A single cloud hung in the air.
It was the dawn of dreams.

The enchantress sky
made it impossible
for me to acknowledge
the dying body in my arms.

But I had to look down.
We all do.

She stared into my eyes, and I
knew that, in that moment, she was
seeing beyond my mortal world.
I had forgotten the pretty shade
of grey that was her soul.

I wish I had looked deeper into it
when time was mine, but now it
was hollow, and the regret was
everything but.

Her dying voice rose up like
the moon. She said,

"Baby, you've been alone for
so long, and now the abyss of
time is dry and I along with it.

The earth is now your hell.

Your pursuit of glory
has left you incomplete,
incomplete and broken.

What have you done?"

You will realize that
happiness, in all its
glory, is not too difficult

a goal if you just stop

asking for the earth.

Simmer down.

Elementary

Some people come
with the cost of
your sanity,

the only cure being distance.

Delinquent

You've truly lost yourself
when you can't blame the
devil anymore,

when you crawl back to
the sin all on your own.

My Demise

Ever since I can remember,
I've never believed in telling
people of my sufferings because
they cannot do anything. They
can listen. They can cry with
you. But they can't make it go
away.

So I refuse to *burden* you with
a matter you cannot help simply
because it will lessen my pain.

I am selfish enough.

That's the beauty of it, isn't it?

You get to choose the words.

Black Eden

I went to a funeral today.
As the families and friends,
clad in black, looked down at
their feet in sorrow and supposed
sorrow, I noticed something that shook
me to my core.

No one was referring to the
girl in the ground by her name,
not even by a simple 'her'.
Now she was simply 'the body'.

We are not taught this;
it is innate.

When our eyes close in this world,
whether or not they open in another,
we are only the things we did and the
things we said.

And after the earth swallows us,
there is no redemption,
no forgiveness.

We are stripped even of our names.

You're pushing me to places where
even I won't have the power to stop myself.

Tread with providence.

Intellectual Conversations with a Whimsical Biologist

I said, "But if there's nothing on the other side?
What's the point of all this life,
this happiness, misery, this strife?"

He said, "But if you think of it like this – if this is
the only life we've got, we ought to make the most of it,
be kind, forgive, forget, breathe, and let go.

If there's only blackness on
the other side, then we would
be the ones who'd lived.

If God awaits us, we'll ask Him
to tell us all the secrets
of the universe."

Stars in Every Darkness Save Our Own

It's been quiet, dark, and lonely.

But the silence is my friend.
It has fused with my pain.
The darkness is my light,
and people have been scared
of her for too long to see the beauty
she holds in her misunderstood depths.

And we've decided that for those
like us, solace can only be found
by being the light in the darkness
of others.

Element

I've learnt the hard way
to never begrudge those
who can't do anything for
you – not because they choose
not to, but because it is simply
out of their reach.

Cloudless

If I hadn't fallen to my
lowest and darkest, I
wouldn't have found this
overwhelming desire to fight back.

Tetrodotoxin

Do not resent poisonous people.
Pity them. They rip and tear men
down, affliction their oxygen.

But on the grand scale of things,
their greatest victims are themselves.

Itch

What is
this ache
I can't
seem to
identify,
or address,
or pity, or
overcome?

Frame of Reference

It's amazing
how a few
short words,
even if small
and insignificant,
can change your
whole perception
of others.

Syria

Leave the bloodstains and the shrapnel,
the rubble and the ruins,
the holes in the walls.

Don't let the world forget.

For Maggie Steber

Sometimes worlds fall apart.
And that is an understatement
in every way possible. But.
In pain and even in death,
there are these fleeting
moments of beauty that
you can only see if you
choose to.
Don't take too long, don't blink,
because if you do, like birds,
they will escape, and you will
never see them again.

It is the *audacity* of beauty to
exist in places of so much
sorrow and heartache and flirt
with our feelings.

Let them make you hopeful.

To My First and Last King

When I was one and when I was two,
and when I was four and when I was five,
I don't remember the things I used to say,
or the things I used to feel,
or the memories that I made.

But there is a man who does.
He knows a part of me that I'll
never know myself.

And that, in itself, is so much.

When I wander and lose myself in these woods,
I will remember you, and I'll find the sea.

Under the sun or under the clouds,
you will hold me, and I will be home.

The Audacity of Beauty II

Like scarlet petunias
and brown sparrows

inside prison walls

Indoctrination

The worst lies are those
we tell ourselves so many
times that the truth slowly
ceases to exist and our reality
becomes a distortion of what is true.

For Hyb

Hey, you,
beautiful, imperfect you.

I've lost grip
over my own mind,
and you should know –
you, precious and rare,
are one of the few things
I've been able to hold onto.
Even when I can't feel myself think,
my will to love and to protect you remains,
strong and unwavering.

Hey, you, beautiful you.
You are perfect in all your imperfections,
flawless in all your flaws.

Your battle makes you glow in my eyes.
You will fall, and you will fall again.
Promise me, promise you will stand tall and never give in.

Hey, you, beautiful you.
Don't take my silence as a message, a message of coldness.
I am trying to hold on by strings of fire,
and you, beautiful you, are one of those strings.

I love you in laughter and in silence,
in my heart and in my eyes,
even when my lips don't move
and my mind wages war on my body.

And if the tides of life carry us away,

I will love you the same.

Tomorrow We Fight Again

When the night blankets the sky
and the world sleeps,
I creep out of my skin and walk
down to the little crevice a little
north of my heart.

In it, the grandfather clock ticks
a little faster than the watch on
my mother's wrist.

In it, everything is covered in dust
and time
except
for the chestnut cupboard.

Bottomless, it only exists in
the blackness if the night
and in the silence of it.

These days, I only open the top drawers,
the things unsettled
[people, their eyes, their words, their lies,
but most significantly, their colours].

At the back lie the things forgotten,
things that will one day find their
way back to me when I least expect it.

The third, the fourth, and the fifth drawers
I do not open – the things settled and what is
left of them [the scars and the lessons, my treasure].

The bottom drawer I can always open, but don't.
When the phantoms of all the things evil plot and
are plotted,

they lurk in corners hidden,
seeping out (on occasion)
in little cascades.

But the art of the matter is that
I have learned to contain, to lock
away, to master [myself] things
that are to be hidden.

Smiling, I withdraw.

Explication

Look into the mirror.
Maybe the person
solemnly looking back
at you is the cause *and the solution*
to the torment you
have been living in.

Talk.

Befriend.

Resolve.

Grow.

Kinda tired.
Kinda feel like *conquering* the world.

Breaking

The things we do carry much more weight
than the things we say.

And that is why sometimes our words
can't take back the things we did.

The good news: people forget what you did to them.

The bad news: they never forget how you made them feel.

Decorum

To be strong in the
presence of others
is precious and rare,

but to be strong
when alone is
a violent art
only few can
tame.

Rubies

Everyone can
listen when you
talk,

but it is the
rare few that
hear you.

Alas, those hearts we crave,
but can only dream of from
distances untold.

Endurance

If you have the consciousness
to feel *guilty* about some of the
things you have become,

I promise you,

you have the power to change,
despite how impossible your heart
and mind always makes it sound
and seem.

Idle

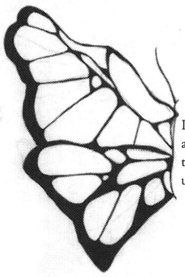

I see your wings,
and it terrifies me
that you may never
use them.

Expressing the Inexpressible

I have found that I am most
inclined to write when feeling
such intricate complexities
become understatements.

You Cannot Give What You Do Not Have

If you wish not to aid
the spread of ache and
mischief in this world,

just remember:

you cannot give
what
you do not have.

So do not harbour in your hearts
hate, nor envy, nor resentment,

and you will not be able to give
such blackness to the world.

Letters from Johannesburg

When time has passed,
and youth like this is a
thing of the past, I hope
that the few that knew
me a little more than I
know myself will look
back and remember me
not as a roadside motel,

but as a home.

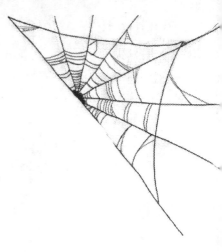

Echo

Maybe I'm so cautious
of how treacherous
people can be because
the same treachery lies
malignant in my own depths.

Bad things are bound to happen.
They carry around them this bizarre sentiment
that makes you believe that they will never leave you.

Give it time, but not years.

Give it tears.
Give it salt, but not pity.
Give it grace.

And one day, when you have
mastered the mystical art of
dominating this pain, this mayhem,
you will whisper to yourself in
silent triumph,

"This is the day I was liberated."

Realism

In our world,
there is no
concept of *unconditional.*

There is simply no such thing.

What is real are circumstances
and those who choose you
over them.

And there are times when
circumstances are chosen over
you.

Precedence

Judge not a man,
for you know not
where he stands.

If you choose to
speak, be **preachers**,

not judges.

Underestimated

In your greatest pains
lie your greatest powers.

In purple darkness, and
as you writhe in the fire
of earthly hell,

do not let go.

The days worth living lie ahead.

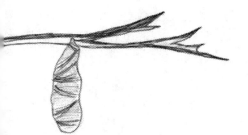

Verdict

After the blood
and the thorns,
the vultures and
the Great War,

I chose to love,
and I rose.

Solace

And if you choose to leave,
I will let you leave.

For I believe in fate and its creator
more than I ever will in any of his mortals.

Selfish

Sometimes we feel like we're not being given
enough space to be who we were born to be.
In those moments, we must rise above ourselves
and acknowledge that people fight their own
battles inside every day just like us. They may
have been patient for you, and now it may be
your turn to give them the space and time they
have been in need of ever since they joined the war.

But if you can't, leave.
Save yourself, and save them the pain.

If someone heals you
as quick as they kill you,

they're poison.

The Self

Injustice, you gave.

And in return, you asked for *love*.

"And Never Is Your Lord Forgetful" [19:64]

I am not one to linger.
I refuse to give up even
the smallest fraction of
my time for hate and for
grudges and for envy.
It's too short a life.

But for you, I will make an exception.

You will wake up in the darkness.
And the horrors that will be your
reality I will not explain.
For they will be yours to know
very soon.

The law I do not hold in my hands.
He holds it.

I could not have asked for a greater justice.

Dimension 4

We are surrounded by things
that are either too big for our
minds to comprehend
or too small for our eyes
to allow to exist,
or by things that
are so far away we'll only
ever know them as numbers.

So, marvel.

Marvel at what you can see.
Because it may be a world
that may not exist to many,

        as so many worlds do not exist for you.

Cages on the Trees of Heaven

It pains me to see the oppressed in this free world,

whose hearts move with everyone else's,

making them forget about the

one lying under their own ribs.

They are stripped of their voices

as their tongues run free.

Native

Forgive me even for the words that
didn't slip off the tip of my tongue,

but rose like tides in my heart.

God knows what is inside is
usually far worse than what
can be expressed.

Limits

Some memories you don't forget.
They are seared into your memory
and become a part of your mind
and prevail above all else.

I let them thrive and pull **me into**
their waters for a while,
but never do I let them drag me
to their depths and silence me whole.

For fragile is something that I am **not**.

Glorious

The Loudest Most Peaceful Silence I Know

When there is nowhere to go,
I am grateful for my mind,
where loyalty is a constant
and betrayal is not feared,
where my thoughts are born
and where I alone reign.

Inborn

Why do we look *up* at the stars
when we long for *home*?

Flurry

Haste, the epicentre of the quake –

let time work its magic, steady,

and allow yourself to *see*
before diving into the vastness.

Abstract

All around people express love
in distances and in levels.
But love, like time and like gravity,
is immeasurable.
It's either there or it is not.

(for us mortals, anyway)

And the artistry is that
the universe and all
its inhabitants
love in all their own
rare and *different* ways.

No levels, no distances required.

Fingerprints

It gives my soul endless solace
in knowing that no matter how hard
anyone tries, that no matter how much
they love me or how much I love them,
they will never understand my pain, just like
I will never understand theirs.

But they can hold me in their warmth,
and I will hold them in mine.

And He,
blissfully aware of our pain,

he will hold us both in His.

Unadulterated

She was the first person I had met who hated fireworks.
She said they were loud and arrogant.

She explained.

As the people kissed and danced under them,
the birds were awoken, and their little hearts
became frightened and their feathered bodies startled.

It was disregard to those we share the earth with.

How human of us, she sighed.

For Letting Us In

I love these words.
I love how I can
read them in the
silence of my mind,

but hear the echoes
of the hearts of all

these writers,
all these poets,
all these artists

whose journeys I have
had the honour to share.

Thank you.

Purpose

Are we just vessels whose sole purpose is to
disperse genetic information to the generations?
Disposable shells?

Are we here because of the random?

No.

I refuse to believe that all this baffling
complexity within us, and in the oceans
and in the forests and in the volcanoes,

all this pain and suffering and heartbreak and words,

all this joy, all the light rays that shine through the branches,

all this intricacy, all this intimacy,

are simply the products of

random.

No.

I Won't Tell a Soul

Trust in me – confide in me. I hold
secrets for the universe herself.

And when I return to the clay and the earth breaks me down,

only then it may find those secrets that
were woven into my existence,

untouched as promised.

Little Mighty

You have come a long way.
I know because I know
            a *truth*.

       It is that we, all who have come before us,
            all that stand now,
         and all that will stand tomorrow,

     were born with storms in our bones, embedded

     with deadly tides that flow in our blood, unstoppable,

         with nebulas in our chests
         and helium hearts, volatile.

And before anyone could rest their gaze
on these storms and killer tides,
you held them by their necks,
and you chained them by their feet, and you
locked away in them what was not meant for
eyes and ears that were not yours.

You didn't even know you had done
what people die doing.

And this is how I know you have come a longer way than most.

Los trapos sucios se lavan en casa.

Origins

When you look back
at the person you
used to be,

don't look down on her,
don't look down on him.

Even if they were as treacherous as the pharaohs,
even if they were as weak as the sparrows,
or even if they were as kind as the sun herself,

they made you the woman you are today,
they made you the man you are today.

If you stand on top of the iceberg in this moment of time,
it is because you were once in the darkness of its depths,

and you chose to rise.

Damaged Goods

When they stop showing
you the respect (the kind
everyone deserves), continue to
respect them, because we
ought to speak to them with
our own words and not theirs.

In your hearts, when they fall
from the ranks, that is truly what
is completely,
utterly,
hopelessly

irreparable.

Ruins

There is this beautiful,
innate feeling that we
humans have that foreshadows
the coming of something terrible.

It is as if the air around us
starts to murmur the
coming of a storm.

I felt it before I met you.

unfortunately, its warnings
were only brought to my attention
after the storm had passed and all that
was left were
ruins.

Genuine

I hope that, when I leave your hand,

you will be capable of seeing the

scarce (and very rare) kindness

that the people harbour in their depths —

like fireflies against the great canvas

of the dark sky, isolated and few.

And I pray that you will not lose hope

when you see the world for what it

truly is.

War of Words

Quite overwhelming when the universe within
the words we so carelessly utter sinks in. As we
effortlessly wisp them out of our flowing mouths
like do magicians with colourful string, we forget
the gravity of which they are made of. That gravity
that has the power to enslave the man, but also to
liberate him. How beautiful, how menacing, how
delicate, how volatile is the power we hold between
our two lips, and how heedless he was of the universe
he had been *entrusted* with.

Polar

When they spoke,
their words cut like
knives,
bitter as the blackest coffee.

But it *reeked* of love
and timeless understanding
of each other,

and that was how I knew
they would find their way.

Repeat one hundred times:

I do not expect anything from you.
You were born to disappoint.

Painful Loyalty

Her imperium was
being able to stand as
tall and as graceful as
the cherry blossoms
after her roots were
used and ripped out
by hands that had
promised
to love.

Her power was dying every
winter, being buried under
the darkness of the white snow
but always coming back with
the spring winds.

It was smiling when the
flowers took her water,
leaving her barren.

Her power was silent, selfless solidarity.

Test

I struggled to know if it
was the real kind of love

or the real kind of
lust.

But I suppose if someone
is willing to wait an
eternity for you,

it must be the deepest possible
kind of that actual kind of

respect

admiration

&

love.

Like good news after war

– that's how I feel about you.

The Cosmos in Me

I may never get to hold you,
but if you will ever be mine
to whisper to,
I'll make sure that you know all the things
I learned in my life, my storm.
My blood will race in your veins.

I will teach you how important it is to be *considerate*.
I fear I won't ever be able to show you the depth
(as complex as the cosmos)
of being able to smile for those you love
even when you're being tormented inside,
to be brave enough to put everyone before you
but to know when to stop.

I will teach you the power of silence and
the power of the unbridled truth.
I will teach you
to dance in your
own raw beauty.
I will teach you to
love like no one ever
taught me.
And above all,
I will teach you
how to teach others.

I will do that and so much
more only by making
sure you know
that you are loved
and that you are not alone.

Intrepid

What is the bravest thing
a human could ever do?

It is no bullet nor mountain.

It is giving someone the key
    to your subtleties, your weaknesses,
it is giving to another the power
to rip you apart but trusting that
they will not.
It is allowing yourself to feel as
deep as the Atlantic for a human
who is impermanent, one who
can perish without warning.

It is making yourself vulnerable
to the most destructive of things.

It is loving.

Conflict

You cannot believe
in coincidence if you
believe in *fate*.

Hijab

Humans

praise flowers
for how they look,
something the flowers
did not determine.

But never for the flower's
ability to stand tall in the
eye of the storm,

to not wilt.

A Tragedy

They say time heals all.
But all it does is make
the wounds feel comfortable
in your skin, so much so
that it wouldn't feel like
home without them.

Powerless

You sit under the sun,
sipping her energy,
telling yourself you will
be stronger tomorrow,
that you and only you
will govern the state
of the beating muscle
in your chest.
You smile.

It takes one look.

       And you watch
yourself unravel,
coming undone.

Ringleader

How can I trust my own mind,
when I have given it every authority
to justify any wrong if it is tempting enough?

Metaphorical

Inside you,
all the hydrogen atoms
are colliding
(620 million metric tons per second).
Inside you,
there is unrest,
there is noise –
a holy mess.

On the gentle surface,
calm and steady,
you shine.

And the roots are
made to grow,
the plants to rise,

the mouths, fed,
the eyes, enlivened,
and the hearts
made serene.

You remind me of the sun.

I

want

you

to

know

you're

stronger

than

your

demons.

Pandemonium

In humans,
at the height of our extremities,
we sometimes lose the ability
to tell the difference between
our emotions.
This is often why we **don't mean**
the things we say in **extreme elation**
or in extreme outrage.

It is also why **maybe we should never**
allow ourselves to go **to places where**
we lose control of our hearts.

Is my heart aching for you out of love,
or is it aching out of unrelenting hatred?

I plan to hold you with love,
then to kill you with my words,
to make you suffer the worst of this world

More

We've got the eyes to marvel at
fields of daisies after it has rained,
the ears to listen to gushing rivers,
the hearts that beat only for us,
and our beautiful paradox of a mind
that is so silent yet so loud.

It makes me sad that the whole world
will never be enough.

Like a Clay Pigeon

I was walking down the stairs,
and that's when I saw her.

She was kneeling before a
girl who wept and wailed.

Her warrior face was overcome
with blatant concern,
and in her beautiful eyes
there was this unadulterated genuineness

that I have come to so deeply love.

But she whose heart moved
with the stranger's struggle –

who will hold her when she needs to be held?
Who will kneel for her like she kneels for the masses?
Who will fight for her when she needs to be fought for?

My darling, you save everyone,
but who saves you?

J.

I pray to God

that you find

someone who

loves you as

fiercely and

as completely

as I wanted to

when the waves

kept me back.

Letters from Mexico
(inspired by a Mexican proverb)

I used to sing the blues because of you.
I used to stare into the vigilant black
of the ceaseless night
and ask God to lift your beastly soul.

But now, I call you back.
I want to express my gratitude to you.
Thank you for burying me deep into the soil.
Without you, I would have stayed there
and never have realized that I was born to
be a *dauntless and defiant seed of God.*

Beacon of bravery for the weak,
pillar of strength for the broken,
ambitions running high,
prospects ready to fly –

hollow inside.

Letters from a Durrani

You can't win this time.

I'm ready to die.

And you,
you are desperate
to live.

Glad You Left

You told me once that people forget what you said, they forget
everything about you at some point, but they never forget how
they felt around you. So, you told me
to tread carefully – to hold
my tongue and to never allow it to scar
people because you knew
how my words cut deep, to lower my gaze, to respect myself by
maintaining my demeanour, not because
it was bad, but because this
world plucks away all the fight in you
as soon as it sees a glimmer
of vulnerability.

And then you left.

I never got to tell you that
all the things you taught me were what
allowed me to grow with grace in a storm so big.

But you already knew the weight of your words, didn't you?

Letters from Constantinople

Some will try to make you jealous.
Others will carefully place thorns
in your path,
throwing their hands into the air,
asking God to curse your existence.
They may even put their heads to
the ground in desperation.

My revenge?

I will survive.

Letters from Balochistan

"What about all those promises you made?"

We must remember
that when the forest
catches fire, it destroys
everything, discriminating
against nothing,

not even the wood
that let it thrive.

Gravitation

"How can you love
a being so sad?"
she asked.

I told her that
I've come to
know that,
surely, it's
the hearts
that we just
cannot ignore.

What Have We Done

You think you look repulsive,
so much that it crushes
your soul and will to do.

I want to tell you that you're
beautiful in your own skin,
only because you are,
and only because everyone
is beautiful in their own skin.

But there is something greater
than looking beautiful.
We worry so much about how
we look on the outside that
we've slowly lost sight of
who we really are inside.

Do we worry about how our
hearts are governed by
hate and jealousy like
we do about the
blemishes?

Do we break down when we
see how we are so full of
ingratitude towards
every blessing,

how we're always on
the quest for
more?

Do we feel disgusted with ourselves
when we realize that everything we
do is to please the masses?

Do we regret the way we
talk to our mothers,
those who love us illimitably,
who we take for granted?

Does it scare us how we
walk upon God's green earth
with arrogance and pride?

Do we worry that we don't love enough,
or that we are destroying ourselves
by telling ourselves we're good enough?

Just Don't Forget Your Roots

Stop.

Feel the clothes
touching your body.

Feel the earth
beneath your feet.

Feel the air
flooding your lungs.

This life is yours.

Let the power of those
words resonate in
your chest.

Tomorrow
you are new.

Forgive,
forget,
love,

&

live.

Forgiveness

The whole world
can stand together
and tell you that you
deserve happiness
on an endless scale.

You may have done
ninety-nine things right,

but there's that one person
(who has found refuge in
the back of your mind)
you absolutely ruined.
There's that one word,
that one thought,
that one deed
you wish you
could erase as if it
were written on
sand.

But it is embedded
in amber,

and it will remain even
after you do not.

We are taught to
forgive our enemies,

but we are not taught
to forgive ourselves.

Not All the Broken Need Saving

How in the dark she would shake
as the river Ravi flowed from her
eyes and onto the earth.

And she felt every feeling, and
as she felt nothing,

and as she put her head to the ground
in complete submission – a position
where man is at his most vulnerable
(and also the position from which
power *blooms*) –
she screamed in all the colours of agony.

And after sustenance and strength descended divinely,

she rose with the grace of a queen,
and she braved the Earth
as though she had never kneeled,
as if she had never allowed rivers
to flow in streams down her face,

as though she had never bled the colour red.

I will not be the victim of my own story.

Power is

killing the evil when
it is inside before it
is outside.

Slates

Some are born on the ground,
others on the hills,
others on the mountains,
and others on the clouds.

And not all of us are taught to dream.
Many are not even allowed to.

And they say we were born equal.

Heart and soul
split into two –
one for nothing,
and one for you.

Scarcity

I do not demand diamonds –
carbon and earth,
abundant and material.

I do not wait for flowers.
Stolen life need not
grace my walls.

I ask for you,
whole and raw.
For there is only one
of that,

and I want it.

Blue Sky

For the grandparents who
don't cross our minds as
often as they should.

*

You may have forgotten
my name, or that your
blood runs in my veins.

But we forgot you before
our brains started to disintegrate.

This time does not discriminate.
It sheds us like feathers when
we fall weak, sometimes even
before our hearts stop beating.

But in the midst of such
lightless realities, of such
urgency, shimmer little
delicacies:

Daadi, in my mother's womb,
I fell heir to your cleft chin.

Now even when this tide
steals you away, it can never
have this part of me — this part
of you that has become a part of me.

*

One day, when our children
forget us, we will not complain.

Ultimate Consumer

If you have taken the
liberty of sharing your
problems with someone
and making them theirs, too,

adopt the decency to include
them in your happiness when
the solution finds you.

Totka

My father decorated
our walls with my
medals and the shelves
with the trophies –
gold and silver and
audacious.

But what he hung
above all were my
failures.

"Meri beti, don't let this gold
and praise fool you. Glory stems
from failing. From failing hard. And
from learning even harder. When you
fall, smile your secret smile and know
that you have been blessed with that
which is immeasurable and vast."

After the sun
comes up, don't
try to find me
where you left me.

I'm not there anymore.

Prowess

I will wear this chaos inside

where no one has to see –

where I fight fire-breathing

dragons and tyrannical voices,

endless black (and myself),

where I change the colours

of my world against

my oppressors.

No one has to know.

To them, I was always whole.

Allegiance

Before
your
words
started
to
feel
like
sweet
syrup
on
my
skin,

I
was
having
dreams
of
you
burying
knives
into
my
spine.

My
heart
always
knew.

311

The most complex,
the most frustrating,
the most beautiful
worldly entity that
I have encountered
is the human brain.

When I feel that I
have understood it
a little better, it is
actually just that I
have stumbled upon a
thousand and one
more layers of
complexity.

*

Today I found out
why we fall in love
with the people that
we do. Or why we feel like
we've known some for a
lifetime when we've only
just met. Or why we get
lost in pieces of art.

You see, our labyrinthine
mind feels a lot. A lot of
overwhelmingly
incomprehensible
heat and loudness.

It then tricks us into ignoring
these presences because they
are simply too tedious to even
begin to comprehend.

Henceforth, when we catch a
glimmer of these deeply buried
intricacies in another soul, our
heart recognizes it and decides
to label it *love*.

We fall in love, mostly with
our own missing pieces, all what
we were never allowed to feel.

We fall in love with the familiar.

Across the River

We were there.

Now we are here.

In between, there
lies a broken bridge
over calm waters.

Though we cannot
return, I'm grateful
I can sit on these shores
on the blue days and
look across the water
at a life that could've been.

Trust Not the Words of Poets

I asked my heart
what it was trying
to say, and it gave
me some words.
Those words I
lent to you. Lent,
not gave. Lent,
not gave. They
are not yours to
give away, not
yours to distort,
not yours to rip
apart in an attempt
to understand them.
They are mine. I made
them. Don't hurt them.
You have the key. Now
don't break into homes that

let you in.

Instead of learning
to become better at
asking for forgiveness,
try doing less of the things
that you must later ask to
be forgiven for.

Predators

You waited till
I was at my
lowest.

Floodgates

If you want to write
(to write good), you
will have to give up
the luxury of blocking
out all the hurt, all the
ache, and all that invites
divine agony. You will
have to let it flow through
your bones, to burn your
insides before you allow it
to pour from the tips of your fingers.

You must allow it to flood.

Miranda

It's too late?

There is no such thing.

It was either meant for you,
or it wasn't.

Let go of what didn't come your
way, and embrace what did.

Flounders

The mountain spring that used
to flow from your eyes
has dried. Though it often
burned your chest with its
ferocity and force, it kept
you sane. It has found a new
home. It is time you did too,
one that doesn't need to feel
like it's setting you on fire
for it to feel like

home.

The June Riots

Do not let anyone
ever tell you that
you are beyond
repair.

There will always
be something among
your ruins that is
worth saving.

Brown Lake

First,
there was
the ringing.

Then came
the silence.

And
I still cannot
decide which
one is louder.

If they could hear the sound
of a woman
breaking,
it would long be a forgotten

tradition.

The Promise

It was March, I believe.
I was on a ferry, floating
on the waters of Istanbul.
I looked out to the sea.
I saw blue.

You walked in.
You walked out.

I looked out to the sea.
I no longer saw the blue.
I saw you.

And never will I see the blue again.

Logastellus

Drown me in
these big,
beautiful
words.

Dear God, please.
When they start
slipping away,
when my mind
forgets how to
tame them, let
me slip away
too.

Take me before
you take my words.

If I keep it hidden for
long enough, it will
cease to exist, yes?

Knitting

It's good to write it all down.
Paper doesn't hear us, but it
remembers after we forget.

But sometimes we should
choose to write about good
coffee, or cats, or that amazing
sound of crunching grave, or the
smell of earth after it rains,
or good books – or phenomenal books,

instead of ache and heartbreak,
instead of toxic people,
instead of poison words,
instead of ugly feelings.

Sometimes it is just
better for all this
healing.

The End

&

A New Beginning

Afterword

For those of us who are exploding
inside with all of the unsaid,
there is God, there is ink, and there is heart.

Printed in the United States
By Bookmasters